Publishing by Liberum Vox Books Ltd

Project by: Liberum Vox Books Ltd
Text and illustrations: Judit Franch
Spanish into English translation: I&K Translations
Review: Julia Gibbs

English translation © Liberum Vox Books Ltd 2016
www.liberumvoxbooks.com

First edition
ISBN: 978-1-910650-02-8

the books about

the Little Lightning Bug's journey

Mum dreams about a Little Lightning Bug

Judit Franch

Liberum Vox
B O O K S

*To the Little Lightning Bug
that brings light into Mum's heart*

Every night
for a very long time,
a Little Lightning Bug
visited Mum in her dreams.

"Tick tock! Tick
tock!" –he insisted
and insisted again and
again in Mum's head–
"I want to be a baby!"

Mum told him:
"Relax, it's not
time yet, later."

But time went on and on,
and the Little Lightning Bug
was getting impatient
and was becoming
more and more insistent.
Mum tried to explain that it
was necessary to wait
a little while longer.

Until one night, the Little Lightning Bug, tired of waiting, started to blow. First he blew very gently, and Mum felt a tingle in her ear, and after that he blew a little harder, and then Mum sneezed. Then the Little Lightning Bug, who was already red from anger, took a deep, deep breath and then blew all the air out, for a *looong, looong,* time...

Air started to swirl
around Mum's head,
and like a hurricane,
moved down to her feet.

Mum, who was sleeping, began dreaming that she was flying higher and higher.

From up there she looked down, and saw that all the obstacles, which had seemed so big before, now looked so small.

Then she felt a sense of peace wash over her and she realised the time had come for the Little Lightning Bug to become a baby.

When she woke up that morning she felt very happy and joyful.

Now, fully awake, she said to herself: "It's time for the Little Lightning Bug to become a baby."

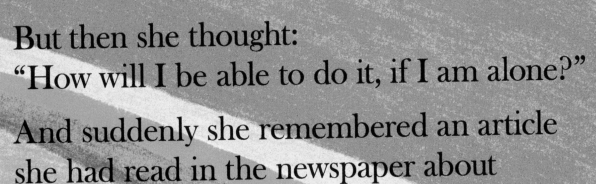

But then she thought:
"How will I be able to do it, if I am alone?"

And suddenly she remembered an article
she had read in the newspaper about
a doctor that helped mums who were
alone to have a baby.

She immediately searched for the
doctor's phone number on the Internet
and asked for an appointment.

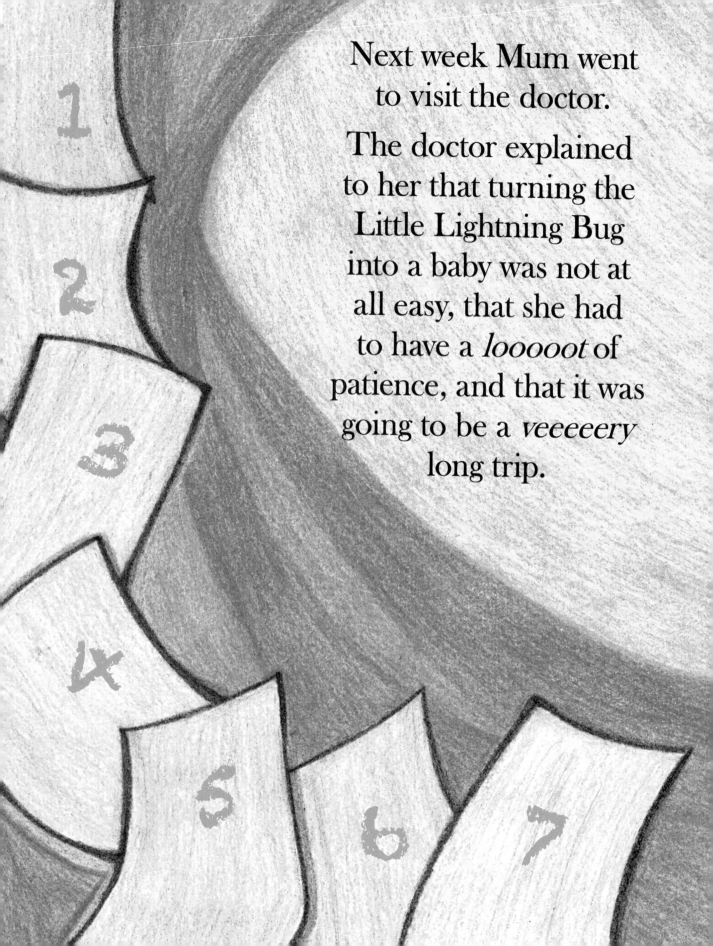

Next week Mum went to visit the doctor.

The doctor explained to her that turning the Little Lightning Bug into a baby was not at all easy, that she had to have a *looooot* of patience, and that it was going to be a *veeeeery* long trip.

1

2

3

4

5

6 7

Mum listened to the doctor's
explanation very carefully,
thought about it for a few seconds,
and said: "I know the difficulties
that must be overcome, but I am
ready to start the journey."

The doctor then smiled to herself, and told Mum that to make a baby you need to put two parts together: one part is called the egg (that women have) and another part is called the sperm (that men have).

And then she added:
"At the Semen Bank, the place where all the Mr Donors come to leave their little seeds (the sperm), I am sure we will find some that is right for you."

1, 2, 3 days... one week...
and the phone didn't ring...
8, 9, 10 days... two weeks and...

It was the doctor, to tell Mum that
the results of the analysis were
good, and that Mr Biologist had
put away a little seed (sperm) at
the semen bank that was perfect
for her.

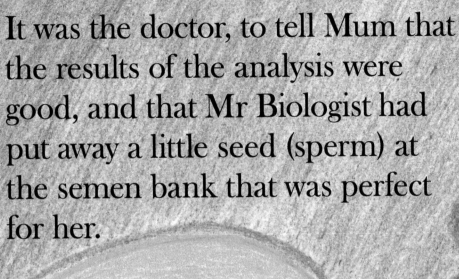

...Ring!
Ring!

Mum's heart
jumped for joy.
She was very
nervous,
excited and
happy!

Mum went to visit the doctor again.
She explained to her that there are
several ways to join the egg to the sperm.
We call this fertilization.

She also told her how they would do it in her case, and that if everything went OK then a zygote would be formed and stay in her belly, and there it would grow for nine long months...
Until a baby was born!

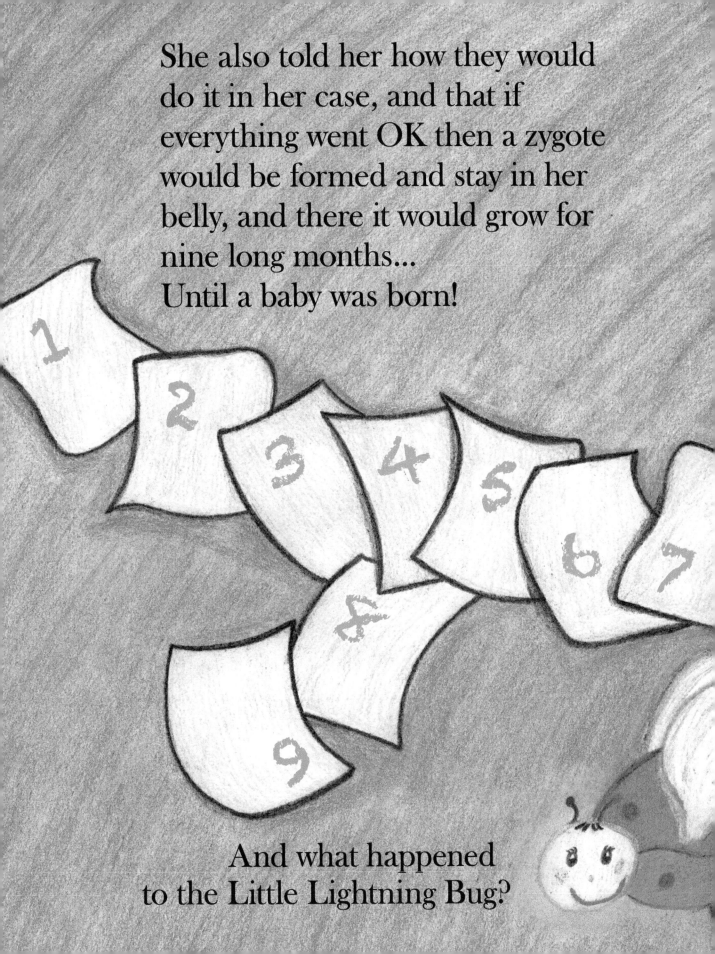

And what happened to the Little Lightning Bug?

...it just so happened that the Little Lightning Bug felt so comfortable in Mum's belly that he grew and grew for... nine months!

And after nine months, when he couldn't possibly grow anymore inside Mum's belly...

who was born?

Glue your photo

End